Great Britain
For Kids
People, Places and Cultures
Children Explore The World Books

SPEEDY
PUBLISHING

Speedy Publishing LLC
40 E. Main St. #1156
Newark, DE 19711
www.speedypublishing.com

Let's learn some interesting facts about Great Britain!

Britain is in north-west Europe and is an island country.

It is made up of three countries England, Wales and Scotland.

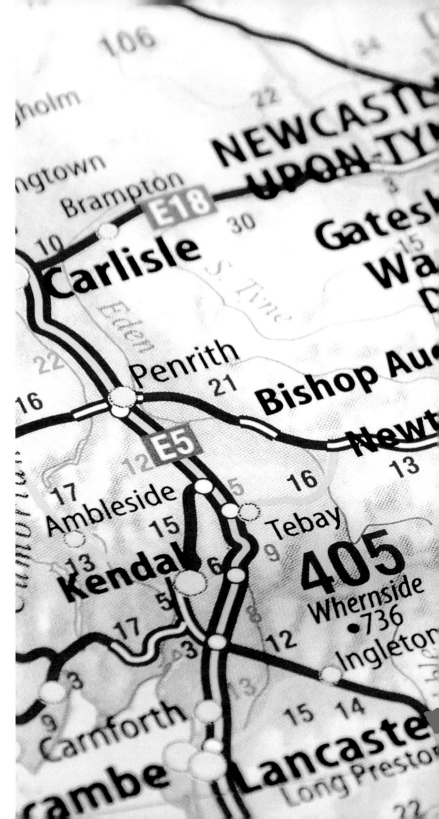

Britain is only 35 km from France and is now linked by a tunnel under the English Channel.

England is the most populated country in the United Kingdom.

The longest river found entirely in England is the River Thames, it flows through London and is slightly shorter than the River Severn at around 346 kilometres (215 miles) in length.

The largest lake in England is named Windermere.

The highest mountain in England is Scafell Pike, which stands at around 978 metres (3,209 ft) in height.

Wales is called Cymru in Welsh.

Wales is often termed "the land of song" the country is known for its harpists, male choirs, and solo artists.

The country of Wales is said to contain more castles per square mile than any other country in the world.

Lamb is the meat traditionally associated with Welsh cooking owing to the amount of sheep farming in the country.

Scotland is located in Europe, at the northern end of Great Britain.

The highest mountain in Scotland is Ben Nevis which stands at a height of 1344 metres (4409 feet).

Scottish drivers use the left-hand side of the road.

Scotland has a unique culture with traditions such as bagpipes, kilts and highland dancing.

The longest river in the United Kingdom is the River Severn. Located in England and Wales, it stretches around 354 kilometres (220 miles) in length.

The official London home of the British monarch (king or queen) is Buckingham Palace.

Great Britain has a lot to offer and you should visit the country soon and explore!

Made in the USA
Lexington, KY
14 April 2019